D1395257

ALEXEI SAYLE'S IMAGINARY SANDWICH BAR

ALEXEI SAYLE'S

Imaginary Sandwich Bar

BLOOMSBURY

LONDON · OXFORD · NEW YORK · NEW DELHI · SYDNEY

Bloomsbury Publishing
An imprint of Bloomsbury Publishing Plc

50 Bedford Square   1385 Broadway
London   New York
WC1B 3DP   NY 10018
UK   USA

www.bloomsbury.com

BLOOMSBURY and the Diana logo are trademarks of Bloomsbury Publishing Plc

First published in Great Britain 2017

© Alexei Sayle, 2017
Illustrations © Andrew Joyce, 2017
The BBC word mark and BBC Radio 4 logo are trademarks of the British Broadcasting Corporation
and used under licence. BBC Logo © BBC 2005. Radio 4 Logo © BBC 2011

British Library Cataloguing-in-Publication Data
A catalogue record for this book is available from the British Library.

ISBN: HB: 978-1-4088-9582-5
          EPUB: 978-1-4088-9584-9

2 4 6 8 10 9 7 5 3 1

Typeset by Integra Software Services Pvt. Ltd.
Printed and bound in Great Britain by CPI Group (UK) Ltd, Croydon CR0 4YY

MIX
Paper from
responsible sources
FSC® C020471

To find out more about our authors and books visit www.bloomsbury.com.
Here you will find extracts, author interviews, details of forthcoming
events and the option to sign up for our newsletters.

To Linda

Chapter One

BAKED POTATOES

Welcome, what can I get you? This sandwich bar that I own and run is clearly imaginary but that is not to say that it doesn't exist, it just exists in a place that is imaginary. You may think this is just comedy bollocks, but there are some modern philosophers who consider that what we think of as the 'actual world' is only one of many distinct possible worlds, so a world where I really do own a sandwich bar is a distinct possible world (though I imagine hygiene standards are a lot lower in that world).

The idea of possible worlds is most commonly attributed to seventeenth-century philosopher and polymath Gottfried Leibniz, who spoke of possible worlds as ideas in the mind of God and used the notion to argue that our actually created world must be 'the best of all possible worlds'. Arthur Schopenhauer argued that, on the contrary, our world must be the worst of all possible worlds, because if it were only a little worse it could not continue to exist. So if you feel your life couldn't get any worse, blame Arthur Schopenhauer.

In the 1960s American philosopher David Lewis went much further and maintained that 'possible worlds' are multiple, really existing worlds, which are simply beyond the one we live in. Lewis argued that these worlds exist just as unequivocally as our actual world, but are distinguished from it simply by standing in no spatial, temporal or causal relation to it. According to Lewis, the only 'special' property that our world has is that we exist in it. You won't get this in any other Christmas book.

1968, A YEAR THAT CHANGED EVERYTHING EVERYWHERE APART FROM IN SOME BITS OF LEEDS

I have been telling people I run a sandwich bar since the mid-1970s. Sometimes my delivery would make it clear that I was joking but on other occasions I would present it as a fact. Pretending to run a sandwich bar combined two of my favourite things, which are pretending and places that sell sandwiches.

It can be difficult to pinpoint exactly when something happened that created an obsession in you or forged a personality trait. The precise moment when Picasso turned to Cubism or Simon Cowell became a bastard are not recorded, but I can tell you exactly when I fell in love with establishments dedicated exclusively to the sale of edible stuff between slices of bread. It was 1968, Holborn in central London, and I was sixteen years old, visiting friends who were appearing in a National Youth Theatre production at a nearby venue. It seems such a long time ago now but it's hard to describe how terrible food was in those days.

These days my home town, Liverpool, is full of great boutique hotels and smart, innovative restaurants, but back when I was growing up in the 1950s and 1960s, the city had a more negative and complex relationship with food. At school a lot of kids were 'fussy eaters': one wouldn't eat peas, another would only eat metal, another wouldn't eat at all unless the patriarch of the Russian Orthodox Church was present. I remember the local ITV station, Granada, doing vox pops, going round Liverpool city centre in the early 1970s asking people what the worst thing was they had ever eaten and one woman said, 'Fish. Fricking fish … it's fricking disgusting.'

And as far as eating out went, it was a culinary desert, Liverpool. In the late 1970s me and my wife Linda were having a meal in a Greek restaurant on Hardiman Street in Liverpool and we ordered the meze, the hummus and the taramasalata and the tzatziki, and after a couple of minutes the Scouse waitress came back and she said, 'We've run out of pitta, do you want Hovis? Because that's a delicious taste of the Peloponnese, isn't it, Hovis?'

So British food in the 1950s, 1960s and 1970s was terrible in every way, like it's hard now to understand how a salad could be racist! And you had all these homophobic pies. I always resist nostalgia; I think it's a very corrosive emotion, nostalgia; people who lived a hundred years ago were never nostalgic, which is why their lives were perfect in every possible way ... summers were ten years long and there were dragons and the King of the North was Jon ... no, hang on, that's *Game of Thrones* ... There's a conviction amongst older people that the past was better than the present but I just think the same terrible things that happen now happened then, they just never told you about it! Like in the 1950s the TV news was sixty seconds long and it was presented by one of the Black and White Minstrels.

It's a fact not well known now but rationing went on long, long after the war ended. In fact, I think truth and honesty are still being rationed by the government yark! yark! I mean, from 1939 to 1945 the government had permitted, indeed had positively encouraged men to bayonet people in the guts or set them on fire with flame throwers or bomb their houses from 20,000 feet, but when they came home they couldn't have a tomato until 1957! Till the 1950s all milk production, apart from what was bottled, went to make something called 'government cheese'. Imagine that? Cheese that tasted like Michael Gove.

Working-class families such as ours did not eat out frequently but, when we did, we would do so at the Bon Marché department store or Henderson's, which we thought of as Liverpool's version of Harrods, except Harrods didn't have a department dedicated entirely to the sale of potatoes. When you ate out in the 1950s and 1960s there was a tremendous lack of generosity in both the service and the cuisine. The staff would grudgingly dole out tiny portions of food as if us diners were survivors of a shipwreck who were now crammed into a lifeboat under the baking sun with rescue not expected to arrive for weeks. You always had the feeling that if you tried to get more than your meagre rations the head waiter was going to shoot you with a revolver.

So that was my experience of eating out when in Holborn I came across this amazing place, a sandwich bar that I can remember vividly to this very day. It was on a corner and the large plate-glass window was stacked high with bread rolls studded with caraway seeds. I was reminded of Miranda's words in *The Tempest*: 'Oh brave new world ... that has such bread rolls in 't!' I went inside and saw the fillings, such fillings. I mean, what kind of a deranged genius would thing of mixing bacon with avocado! There was 'Minty Lamb', 'Tuna Mexicaine' and 'Egg'. There was a generosity about it and a lack of formality; no snooty head waiter; you could eat your sandwiches there or you could take them away. I just fell in love with the whole idea of sandwich bars.

'Oh brave new world ... that has such bread rolls in 't!'

IMITATING CHRISTINE WALKER

In 1976 my friend Glen decided to give up advertising to spend a year teaching English in the Sudan. On his return he was supposed to be staying with his brother but they had a row at Heathrow Airport a few minutes after his plane had landed and so Glen phoned and asked if he and his new New Zealander girlfriend Virginia could stop for a short while in our spare room in the council tower block where we lived. When they arrived from the airport dragging several huge, overstuffed suitcases behind them, Glen and Virginia were both painfully thin and their skin was a bright orange hue due to a tropical parasite they had picked up. Both of them spent their first few days back in London in our lavatory, terrible noises issuing from the interior. Me and my wife Linda were so worried about catching the same parasite that we used a toilet in a pub, a bus ride away over the river in Wandsworth.

As the weeks of their stay lengthened, the couple hardly ever went out but remained in the flat all day, arguing with each other and smoking continuously. After a while me and Linda had had enough and we asked Glen and Virginia to move out, but rather than being honest we told them untruthfully that our old friend Christine Walker was coming to stay with us indefinitely and she would be needing the room.

Reluctantly the emaciated couple agreed to move out but asked if they could leave their suitcases behind, since the only place they could find to rent was a tiny bedsit with no storage space. We said yes but this presented us with a problem – one or other of them would be regularly returning to pick stuff up from a room in which Chris Walker was supposedly staying. I therefore felt I had to fake Chris's day-to-day presence.

First of all I got some old shoes of Linda's and scattered them around then threw some clothes about in a similar fashion. Next I placed a book by the bedside, open about halfway through, and beside it a glass of water. When I stood back and surveyed all this it looked incredibly false. Nobody, I thought, would believe that a real person was spending time in this room. There was a need for more detail. Feeling rather strange I put some of Linda's lipstick on, then took a sip of water to leave the imprint around the edge of the glass. That felt better. Finally I took all my clothes off, then I sprayed some old perfume Linda never used over my body, then I got into the bed and rolled around to give it that rumpled look.

Every time Glen or Virginia came back to get something from their cases I would have to make alterations. Turning the pages of Imaginary Chris's bedtime reading, buying her new clothes from the

Oxfam shop to scatter around and leaving a pack of Tampax open once a month, though I was unsure how many of these things women got through each month: two boxes? Five?

Yet I still felt as though there was something lacking from my creation of Imaginary Chris's life, some kind of authenticity. So then I wondered if I shouldn't give her more of a backstory, sort of like when actors in a film create a whole life for the characters they play, even though none of that life is apparent to the audience seeing the film.

So why was she in London? I asked. Who was she friends with? Well in my mind somebody as free and adventurous as Imaginary Chris would have plenty of friends and, I thought, lovers too. I imagined she was having an affair with a married guy from the television company where she worked but Imaginary Chris being the kind of woman she was, would also in the past have slept with women as well as men; you couldn't tie Imaginary Chris down. (Except sometimes Imaginary Chris did like being tied down but only by another woman.) I would have left napkins from lesbian bars lying around if I'd known where any were but instead I wrote a couple of passionate notes in what I hoped was disguised handwriting signing them 'Vicky' and detailing what Vicky would like Imaginary Chris to do to her. These I put in a drawer where Glen or Virginia would never see them but I felt it lent an air of authenticity.

When the couple finally got a bigger place and they came and took their cases away, Imaginary Chris was suddenly no longer necessary. Despite my protests, Linda insisted that I clear the spare room of Chris's things, which made me sad because I missed her terribly, plus there was a definite feeling that there'd been some kind of spark between the two of us.

INSIDER GOSSIP

This book is obviously based on the Radio 4 show of the same name. I like to think of *Alexei Sayle's Imaginary Sandwich Bar* as exactly the type of radio programme that the abbreviation 'WTF' was invented for. And here I'll let you into a little trade secret. If you've ever been to a radio or TV recording you will know that, at the start, before the recording begins, the producer comes out and makes a little speech and gets the audience to practise laughing and clapping several times. At my show we do things differently. My producer comes out and asks the audience to be as lethargic and uninterested as possible then he tells them a long story about his cat's kidney stone operation but still they laugh! Ha ha ha!

BOILED ONION

Because I am a celebrity I also have a lot of celebrity customers at my imaginary sandwich bar. One is Neil Kinnock, once leader of the Labour Party and vice-president of the European Commission. ex-chair of the British Council and former president of Cardiff University, who, when he's attending the House of Lords, comes in for his regular falafel wrap with extra beef gravy and a boiled onion. He's a right bastard, he is, I hate him! I wish I didn't have to serve him and smile so politely, all the time bowing and scraping and saying, 'Yes, sir, no, sir,' and calling him 'mate'. One of these days I'll kill him, so help me I will.

One of my favourite characters in fiction is Pirate Jenny from Brecht's *The Threepenny Opera*. Jenny is a waitress at a 'crummy old hotel', who fantasises that she is in fact a notorious pirate. One morning a pirate ship – with eight sails and fifty guns loaded – sails into the harbour. The pirates come ashore, clap all the townspeople in irons and drag them to Jenny, where they ask, 'Which ones shall we kill?' and she says, 'Hoopla! All of them.' Then she sails away with the pirates. That's how everybody who works in a sandwich bar feels all the time.

Later I was to learn that sandwiches are not just delicious to eat, they can also tell us a lot about history. Their very name, for instance, shows us a lot about the rapaciousness of the British aristocracy: how they appropriate and steal everything they come across. There's this myth that the sandwich was invented by the Earl of Sandwich who was too busy to get up from the card table and instead told his cook to prepare him some meat between two slices of bread. Do you think the Earl of Sandwich was the first person to think of putting a bit of meat between two slices of bread? Hell no! But he's all, 'I invented da ...' By the way, all aristocrats back then spoke in thick Scouse accents. If you visited the royal palace or the Admiralty in the eighteenth century, it would have sounded like a pub in the Merseyside satellite town of Huyton. Therefore it is best if you imagine the Earl of Sandwich's words being spoken by Len McCluskey, General Secretary of Unite the Union, or the actor Ricky Tomlinson. He'd say, 'I'm the fucking Earl of Sandwich, me, and I invented the sandwich and I'm also the Duke of Catflap 'cos I thought of them too. And you can also call me the Marquis of Hovercraft. I invented the hovercraft after I saw one operating a regular service between Portsmouth and the Isle of Wight.' Cos I'm the fucking Marquis of Hovercraft and the Earl of Sandwich, me. Before I invented the sandwich, if people wanted a snack they'd have to eat a football squeezed between two bricks or a dog served between two other bigger dogs or a bowl of muesli, because I'm the Earl of Sandwich!'

Apart from being delicious to eat sandwiches and sandwich fillings can also teach us a lot about history; for example, there is Coronation Chicken. This sandwich filling is named in commemoration of the events of 1878 when following a misprint in the Almanach de Gotha after the death of the King of Prussia, a chicken was crowned as his replacement. That chicken ruled over one of the longest periods of peace and prosperity in northern Europe.

Then there's the Prawn Cocktail. This filling orig-inated in the United States during the era known as Prohibition. At that time the only way to get around the ban on the consumption and sale of alcohol was to disguise your drink as a three-course meal. Hence the development of the Prawn Cocktail (and its less successful siblings, the Beef Martini, the Whitebait Spritzer and the Pork and Soda).

And, finally, Lamb Tikka. The name comes from the period in India during partition when Hindu and Muslim separatists would put alarm-clock-timed bombs inside sheep then drive them into busy marketplaces. 'Lamb Tikka' was often the last thing some poor shopper said before the bomb exploded.

*That chicken ruled over one of the longest periods
of peace and prosperity in Europe*

A LIFE OF PRETENDING

But it wasn't until the mid 1970s I think that I
began actually pretending to run a sandwich bar.
Sometimes I was honest with people and told them
it didn't exist; on other occasions I was less forth-
right. I remember one weekend in 1976, me and
Linda went to the Odeon in Leicester Square to see
the newly released Sylvester Stallone movie *Rocky*.
Before the lights went down, I noticed in the audience a few rows behind me a mournful-looking,
slightly pop-eyed, balding man with a droopy moustache. I whispered to Linda, 'You see that man in

the fifth row? I think it's Walid Jumblatt, leader of the Druze militia from the Chouf Mountains of the Lebanon.'

'You're always saying that,' she replied.

'Yes,' I hissed, 'but this time I'm certain.' The Druze sect were much in the news because they were one of the factions fighting in the Lebanese Civil War.

After the film finished I approached the man with the moustache and said to him, 'Excuse me, are you Walid Jumblatt, leader of the Druze militia from the Chouf Mountains of the Lebanon?'

'Yes I am,' he said.

'What did you think of the film, then?' I asked after a pause.

'It was all right,' he replied.

After I got back to Linda she said, 'Did you tell him about your sandwich bar?'

'Yes, I told him that all races and religions mixed in my sandwich bar without any tension and I wondered if he'd ever thought that the problems in the Middle East might be solved by the installation of a help-yourself salad bar; people never seemed angry when they were going back for a second helping at a salad bar.'

'What did he say to that?'

'He said it seemed a bit simplistic.'

Why did I do it? The pleasure of pretending, I suppose. But what is the impulse to pretend to do something like running a sandwich bar? Well, I personally think, if a job's worth doing, it's worth pretending to do it. Which is not to say that it doesn't require skill and dedication. Like in 1999 I had a role in a British movie called *Swing,* which starred Lisa Stansfield who'd been around the world but she couldn't find her baby (which is really a matter for social services). My part was as the trumpeter of the swing band that she was in. Now I can't play the trumpet, but in the film I acted as if I could. I pretended to play the trumpet and I really really enjoyed pretending to play the trumpet so much and I was good at it too! Sometimes I'd pretend to play the trumpet when the cameras weren't rolling; me and the other actors who also couldn't play their instruments would jam. Now it obviously wasn't as hard as actually playing the trumpet, but there was a certain skill required, I spent minutes practising and I really wished there was a place to go, a club or something where people could come along to watch me pretending to play the trumpet. Maybe if it only cost £1 to get in and there were, like, free T-shirts they might come.

So pretending to run a sandwich bar gave me, I suppose, the pleasure of being someone else, leading a different life but without any of the consequences. It gave me tremendous satisfaction to talk about all my innovative baked-potato toppings and how I was one of the leading lights in the focaccia revolution, even going to the Italian town of Focaccia in the province of Panini to study different recipes. Did you know there'are a town in Southern France called Tourette and when you're driving through there are people on the corner shouting 'Arse!' and 'Bastard!'? No, hang on, that was me.

But now if anybody asks how my sandwich bar is going I find I cannot be optimistic about the business any more. Like small traders everywhere, even in the imaginary world, I am facing competition. Other celebrities are getting in on the act: David Walliams with his chain of imaginary nail salons... no, hang on, that's real. But it's happening in the real world too. For example that sandwich bar in Holborn is still there, but it is now a branch of the chain Pret A Manger. There's this hipster coffee-bar chain called Harris + Hoole, which is actually owned by Cáffé Nero. All the bushy beards their baristas have are just stuck on with glue and they peel them off at night. The restaurant chain Giraffe. The food at Giraffe does not resemble anything you would expect to be given in a restaurant; rather it is what might be served to the inhabitants of a badly run international moon colony – fajita hummus pockets, avocado spring onion doughnuts served on a salsa of stuffed chicken-wing gravy or Romanian-style waffle of teriyaki bacon with Cajun radish fried-crisp explosion. TGI Fridays epitomises the lies that these huge chains are built on because let's face it most of the time it isn't Friday, is it? But the management at head office back in Ohio forces all its employees to pretend it is Friday, every day of the week. If anybody asks what day it is, they have to reply, 'Friday'.

WHERE ARE THEY NOW?

Occasionally, years ago, I would write about my sandwich bar in newspaper columns and, once again, sometimes I mentioned it was imaginary and at other times I didn't. Certainly several people have told me over the years that they'd visited it. I loved having a column in a newspaper and I've worked for quite a few but now they themselves are nearly extinct and I'm sort of sad about that except for all you critics who gave me bad reviews! What are you doing now? Working in a mobile car-valeting service, that's what! While I'm still here. Talking crap about an imaginary sandwich bar on the radio and then having it made into a book! While you've all been replaced by the internet. Ha ha ha!

TAYLOR SWIFT CAN SEE YOU NOW

The internet, Twitter, Instagram, all that, that's what's done for newspapers. I'll tell you who's really good at the internet – the singer Taylor Swift. She does all this stuff like she routinely retweets her followers and comments upon their photos. She also puts up posts on her personal feed of her interactions with her fans. At Christmas, which she renamed #Swiftmas, Taylor left a Santa emoji on the profiles of some fans (which is apparently a good thing) and she actually went out and personally delivered Christmas gifts to a select few of her followers. But what's more interesting is that Taylor Swift also regularly has a few of her fans randomly attacked in the street and beaten up by anonymous assailants, their credit history is wiped out by nameless hackers or, if they're in hospital, their medication gets mysteriously swapped with poison. Because Taylor Swift understands that you cannot have light without darkness, good without bad, yin without yang. This perhaps explains the murder of Alexander Litvinenko in London in 2006 with radioactive polonium. He was like ... just a huge Taylor Swift fan.

Pretending crops up in the oddest places. You know, I have now actually got so fat that I've begun buying my clothes at shops that specialise in garments for the more portly gentleman. A chain of shops that I used to call Mister Fat Bastard. But I thought that there was something odd about the appearance of the man who served me. Then I figured it out. I don't know if you know this but opticians who have perfect sight will still wear spectacles with plain glass in them just to reassure their customers, so it was that I suspected this man was really wearing a false stomach, so that his customers didn't feel self-conscious about their obesity. I myself felt reassured that I was being served by a fatty, even if he was a fake fatty. And that made me think that pretending perhaps plays a more important part in our lives than we acknowledge. For instance, we want our politicians to pretend that they are in control of events, that we are safe and secure, that if we simply vote the right way then things will be fine because they know what they are doing. But the truth is, nobody's in control! Or maybe I was being a harbinger of things to come because these days there is not much that is real. Money isn't real, it is no longer gold or even paper, it's just numbers in a central bank's computer; work isn't real, nothing is made any more, people just spend days in meetings and nobody is who they say they are on the internet, if my experiences on Grindr are anything to go by.

Chapter Two

BARRY AND ANITA

We keep our spare keys in a ceramic pot that I was given years ago by someone who was a first-year pottery student. I was getting some keys out of this jar for a friend.

'That's er … quite ugly,' the friend said of the pot.

'Is it?' I replied. 'I'd stopped noticing how horrible it looks.'

'Then it's a Grunty,' she said.

'A what?' I asked.

'A Grunty. It's something you have in your house that's hideous and useless but you've stopped noticing it completely, so it's effectively invisible.'

I was much taken with this idea and it brought to mind a couple we know whose small living room is more than half taken up by a huge, ugly and quite sickly Swiss cheese plant. Rather than throwing it out, they adapt each time a dangling mangy yellow leaf threatens to block out the picture from their TV by moving the sofa.

As well as Grunties I think there are also Gruntyisms, things you say or do, though the reason why you say or do them has long since been forgotten. For example, every time we drink soup my wife and I always say the same thing; uttered in a strange monotone, we say, 'Soup, swoop, loop de loop.' The way we came to say 'Soup, swoop, loop de loop' every time that we drink soup came about like this. For a married couple the years between your mid thirties and your late forties might be seen as the decade of the bad dinner party. You are no longer looking for a partner so your inclination to visit crowded bars has receded but you are still full of energy so you don't want to stay in at night. So instead you go to dinner parties attended by other couples you don't necessarily like that much. One such couple were called Barry and Anita. Every time we ate at their house, Barry would make soup and when serving it he would invariably say, 'There we are, soup, swoop, loop de loop.' After the dinner party me and Linda would start talking about what an arse Barry was as soon as we were in the minicab going home. We would say to each other in a high-pitched mocking imitation of Barry's voice, 'Soup, swoop, loop de loop,' and, 'Please do have some more of this soup, swoop, loop de loop,' then we would collapse against each other laughing, convincing the Algerian or Bengali taxi driver once again of the impenetrability and corruption of Western society. Pretty soon, when we had soup at home me and Linda would say to each other, 'Soup, swoop, loop de loop,' at first still ridiculing Barry but eventually we forgot why we were saying it and long after we'd gratefully ceased having soupy dinners with Barry and Anita it had become part of the private language that every couple develops.

In the early 1990s we had an exchange student staying with us for a year, a Māori girl from the Southern Pacific Cook Islands who, when she returned home, took the expression 'Soup, swoop, loop de loop' with her and spread it amongst her extended family until finally the phrase appeared in an anthropological dissertation: '"Soup, swoop, loop de loop". Shamanistic Incantations in Rarotongan Food Preparation Rituals', University of Topeka, 2001.

YO-YO WHAT?

Yo-Yo Ma, the famous Chinese-American cellist, came in today for his regular tandoori chicken wing ciabatta roll with parsnips. There's actually an interesting story behind his name. In ancient times in

China the yo-yo, now thought of as a toy, was originally a weapon or a tool for hunting. It was a sort of oriental version of the boomerang but obviously with a shorter range (though there are some legends of giant Han-dynasty war yo-yos that could destroy a city wall). In time, the use of the yo-yo became the exclusive province of certain highly trained martial arts clans and Yo-Yo Ma is the direct descendant of one of these families.

THE REVOLUTIONARY IMPULSE

I'd like to share my thoughts on political belief and pretending. Both my parents were members of the Communist Party of Great Britain. The violent overthrow of capitalism was sort of our family business. I always thought if we'd had a van it would have written on the sides in big letters: 'Joseph Henry Sayle and Son, Revolutionaries. Estimates given, no Kalashnikovs left in this van overnight.' Incidentally, there was a van parked outside my house a while ago from a firm that specialised in blocked drains and particularly sewage clearance and it said on the back door of the van: 'CCTV a speciality. No stools left in this van overnight.' I didn't write it; I'm stealing material off the side of vans! Cricklewood Garage: it was on the side of a bus; I thought it might give you a bit of a laugh.

When I became a teenager, my act of rebellion against my parents was to become more left-wing than them, so I joined a Maoist party. We'd have these rows at the breakfast table:

'Don't you call your mother a revisionist, running-dog lackey, our Lexi.'

'Well she is, Dad, as Chairman Mao says, she's waving the red flag to defeat the red flag!'

But having both my parents as Communists meant I was essentially brought up in a cult. John Maynard Keynes said, 'When the facts change, I change my opinion.' But when you're in a cult, when the facts change, you change the facts! To the end of her life my mother would never admit that there was anything wrong with the Soviet Union. The most she would admit was, 'Mistakes were made.' But as she used to say, 'You can't make an omelette without murdering forty million people.'

The philosophical and ideological basis for Communism, which is Marxism, was essentially created in the nineteenth century in the same place where all the big ideas that would convulse the twentieth century were thought up – i.e., the various principalities and statelets that would later become Germany or the fading Austro-Hungarian Empire. Particularly one city – Vienna. We had Marxism, Freud and psychoanalysis, Einstein, who discovered relativity and the foundations of the nuclear age, Zionism, the idea of a permanent homeland for the Jewish people, and Fascism – I mean there's something there for everybody, don't you think? If you can't find an idea there that appeals to you, I don't know what's wrong with you.

'CARLUCCIO'S!'

My experience of being brought up in this atmosphere of Communism has given me a fascination with people who try and change the world, and the effects that their actions have. Personally I have nothing to do with party politics. Though I remain left-wing, my firmly held conviction has always been that stand-up comedians should have absolutely nothing to do with one political party, no matter how much they might support that party's policies. I am aware that others might not agree. I seem to remember that

Eddie Izzard once had plans to run as Labour Party candidate for Mayor of London (or maybe he was planning to run as mayor of eleven different cities on eleven different consecutive days in aid of Children in Need). Either way, that scheme seems to have gone away. Eddie Izzard runs loads of marathons, doesn't he? Like ten, one after the other. And what I take away from that is that it's a lot easier to run marathons than you think. On the right Jimmy Carr sits in the Storting, the Norwegian Parliament, as an MP for the centre-right Kristent Samlingsparti, the Christian Unity Party (though this may be part of a strategy by Jimmy to try and gain some kind of Europe-wide parliamentary immunity).

Eddie Izzard also does his act in loads of different countries in loads of different languages. I'm thinking of doing that as well. This is the opening bit of my French act: it goes, 'Liberté, égalité, salon de thé!' It's shit, but it's in French! And my Italian act just consists of me shouting 'Carluccio's!' over and over again.

The reason I believe we comics have to steer clear of any and all political parties is that we have a sacred duty to, as the Quakers put it, 'Speak Truth to Power'. (I also shout obscenities at the man who works on the fish counter at Morrisons but that's something different.)

But I want to remain politically engaged so what I do is I involve myself in loads of single-issue causes like homelessness, animal rights ... people sometimes criticise us animal rights activists because we concentrate on fur rather than leather, but I say it's a lot easier to harass an old lady than a biker gang! I cycle everywhere. You've heard of MAMILS, Middle Aged Men in Lycra, well I'm a PUFFIN, a Pathetic, Unfit, Fat Fellow in Nappies. By nappies I mean the huge wodge of foam I have to wear between my legs to stop the razor-thin saddle splitting me in half. And environmental issues: I recycle, and every time I take a flight I plant a tree ... which really annoys the cabin crew!

Pathetic, Unfit, Fat Fellow in Nappies

So as I was saying, I think despite all the chaos we create, the famines, the gulags, left-wing people are basically good people. Admittedly revolutionary left-wing regimes might over time devolve into authoritarian kleptocracies whose autocratic rule is enforced by terror and torture, but we do mean well. We're nice people and sincere in our beliefs, unlike right-wingers. Let's face it, if you're a Tory, say, you're a bit of a bastard. Mildly xenophobic, reactionary, greedy; you don't want others to have what you have and you like golf.

Regardless of the chaos that comes later, we left-wingers at least start out with the intention of bringing a fairer world to more or less everybody, whereas right-wingers are only ever interested in bringing advantage to a narrow group – themselves and people like them. And the further right you go, the nastier people get.

My first volume of memoir, *Stalin Ate My Homework*, was a warm-hearted evocation of growing up in a Communist household. Now you simply couldn't write a warm-hearted evocation of growing up in a Nazi household, could you? 'Dad came in last night hungry for his tea after an evening spent attacking Pakistanis with a claw hammer...' It doesn't work, does it? 'Oh how we laughed when mum used to scream in the streets about the Jews controlling world finance.'

The BNP, the British National Party, were the successors to the Fascist National Front and I actually know a bloke who accidentally hosted a BNP wedding! He had a big historic barn and fields on his land that he rented out for weddings and he took this booking not knowing that the bride and groom and all their friends were in the BNP and he said the thing you noticed was how absolutely horrible they all were! Rude, aggressive, drunken, chippy. And they even had a BNP wedding planner! 'Yes, we'll have a line of SS Stormtroopers scattering petals in front of the bride and groom and the band will play "Tomorrow Belongs To Me" as you make your vows, honest, it'll be gorgeous...'

And apparently stupid too. As well as running my imaginary sandwich bar, I am Pretend Professor of Cognitive Psychology at the University of Uppsala or somewhere. One of the tropes that defines bigots is the absolute certainty they have in their beliefs, right? Now there's this thing in cognitive psychology called the Dunning-Kruger effect. The Dunning-Kruger effect apparently shows that 'low intelligence' is often accompanied by increased confidence in one's opinions and an apparent inability to accurately judge your own abilities and expertise in comparison to others'. Also a willingness to present your poorly thought-out conclusions as cast-iron facts. In other words, the Dunning-Kruger effect proves that stupid people don't know they're stupid! They think they're dead clever! And just to confirm your experiences, if you've had anything to do with BT Broadband, incompetent people don't have the ability to know that they're incompetent – they think they're bleeding great!

In a political sense I find all this very worrying. I have always subscribed to the liberal notion that if you just sat a person with disturbed, anti-social ideas down, somebody such as Hitler or Pol Pot, and talked to them rationally for a long, long time, possibly aided by a chart, a PowerPoint presentation, some maps, a list of statistics and an article written by Simon Jenkins in the *Guardian,* then eventually they would change their minds.

'Oh man,' Pol Pot would say after I'd been going on at him for a bit, 'I see it now, Alexei, that whole Year Zero, Killing Fields thing, oh that was like some messed-up shit, man! Oh I feel so ashamed!'

And Saddam Hussein would have gone, 'Jeeze Louise! Me attacking Iran, oh well, Alexei, that was just plain wrong!'

And Tony Blair would say, 'Oh Alexei, I'm s—', Oh, that's not going to happen ever.

'SHOP TO LET, ENQUIRE AT SHOP NEXT
DOOR'

I'm actually something of a connoisseur of closed-down or closing-down restaurants, because you know it's somebody's dream, isn't it? I've noticed that when a failing café is completely empty, a waiter will always go and stand in the doorway looking up and down the street with an incredibly mournful expression on his face. I reckon if you want to get the punters flocking into your eatery, then stationing a manic depressive in the entrance isn't the right way to go about it.

And, finally, when the place does inevitably go under and they put a handwritten notice in the window saying something like: 'Restaurant closed for redecoration/refurbishment – grand reopening in three weeks', the notice will still be there, yellow and withered with age, several years later.

I don't know why these owners put up the little notice. Is it some pathetic piece of self-delusion or is it, as seems more likely, a feeble attempt to put off all their creditors for a couple more weeks? Either way, nobody pays any attention to the sign. Unlike two rather effective little handwritten signs round the corner from my house. In the Gray's Inn Road there is a stationery shop that has gone bust. In the window is a notice written in felt-tip pen on an old envelope

saying: 'Shop to Let – Enquire at Shop Next Door'.
The shop next door is a halal grocer's, which has also
gone out of business. In its window is another note
in felt-tip saying: 'Shop to Let, Enquire at Shop Next
Door' and an arrow that points straight back to the
empty stationer's. Several times I have seen potential
lessees stuck like wasps against a window, buzzing
backwards and forwards from one sign to another.

Now my imaginary sandwich bar is in the Gray's
Inn Road and shares a building with Channel 4
News and ITN News. I've noticed that whenever
these news programmes do vox pops – you know,
going out onto the streets and asking the public their
opinions on pressing matters of the day – they only
ever go up the road a bit 'cos I always recognise where
there are. In fact I'm often in the back of the shot
making wanker gestures. But they're powerful, these
vox pops, because even though it's only a few random
people, there's a sense that they somehow represent
the wider public. I'm not the only one to remark on
this. So a few years ago I noticed these shops opening in the Gray's Inn Road with names like Taliban
Shoe Repairs and some very keen prices. And then
I'd see these vox pops on Channel 4 News and people
would say things like, 'Well, I profoundly disagree
with the Taliban's medieval and repressive version of
Islam but they did replace the soles and heels on my

black brogues for a very reasonable £6.95 … so, you know, swings and roundabouts, really.'

Or, 'Well, I went to Vladimir Putin's Oak Furniture Land and though he is clearly running a foul kleptocracy that falsely imprisons and murders its critics, there is no veneer used in any of his products, so he can't be all bad.'

You know, people say to us comedians, 'You'll mock evangelical Christianity and you'll take the piss out of Zionism, but you'll never ever really criticise fundamentalist Islam…' Of course not! Those people are bleeding crazy! It's a very overrated virtue, bravery.

I met my wife Linda just before I left Liverpool to go to art school in London. After we'd been going out for a few months I felt I had to tell Linda about my career as a drug dealer. At the age of sixteen, still at school and obsessed with the idea of forging myself some kind of hipster identity, I'd noticed in the pubs, coffee bars and drinking clubs where I spent my evenings that the person with the coolest aura seemed to be the guy selling the dope. He would suddenly appear, then glide about as if on wheels, speaking to his clients in intimate whispers, with all the time hanging over him this romantic, lawless, outsider mystique, and everybody always seemed really pleased to see him.

I was not alone in thinking that drug dealers were the epitome of all that was trendy and hip in the late 1960s. In the film *Easy Rider* the two heroes, role models for a generation, make the money for their doomed motorcycle trip to Mardi Gras from a massive cocaine score. The drugs are hidden in the Stars and Stripes petrol tank of Peter Fonda's bike. This was not seen as a bad thing. Indeed, the influence of this, outlaw drug movie was so far-reaching that the children's bicycle, the Raleigh Chopper, with its enormous chromed handlebars, tiny front wheel and two kilograms of white powder hidden in the frame was clearly based on the Harley-Davidson motorcycles ridden by Peter Fonda and Dennis Hopper in the film.

I really wanted to gain some of the allure of the drug dealer for myself. My feeling was that I had the clothes and the long hair but the only thing that I didn't have was the cheap drugs. From watching movies such as *Easy Rider* and *The French Connection* I understood that one important -- indeed crucial – aspect of being a drug peddler was that you had to have access to reasonably priced narcotics. You got these narcotics from a connection further up the chain, who sold you your product at wholesale prices, and you made a profit from the difference between the price paid by the dealer and what you charged your clients. It was simple Marxist economics, really. My only problem was that I didn't have this connection with a wholesaler, didn't know how to go about getting one and in fact, didn't want to, since I suspected that people further up the chain might be very frightening indeed.

Then it struck me that if I didn't care about making a profit or indeed if I didn't mind sustaining a small loss, then I would be able to sell marijuana or acid at the same price, or maybe even cheaper, than anybody else on the scene. So what I did was, I would buy drugs at the ordinary street price, usually from some guy up the coast in Southport that my friends back in Liverpool knew nothing about, then I'd sell these drugs to people in Liverpool, in the Maoist group I was a member of, or to friends from school, at a price about 15 per cent less than I had paid. I didn't think that Karl Marx in any of his works, not even his *Grundrisse* of 1858, whose subject matter included production, distribution, exchange, alienation, surplus value, labour, capitalism, the rise of technology and automation, pre-capitalist forms of social organisation, and the preconditions for a Communist revolution, covered my particular form of capitalist exploitation, which contradicted every known form of Marxist thought, since the retailer – me – was in effect extracting surplus value from himself. Nevertheless, when customers asked me how I got my drugs so cheap, I'd just look all mysterious and say, 'Hey, I'm like connected with The Man. Know what I mean, dude?' And they'd nod and say, 'Yeah, I understand, man … cool.'

When I told Linda about my cut-price drug dealing, expecting her to be impressed and maybe even a bit horrified at my lawlessness, she said it was the saddest thing she'd ever heard. I replied, 'Yeah, sad if you like having lots of great friends who cost you less than three pounds a week.' But over time I began to suspect that she might have been right.

WHO DARES WINS A COCONUT

Karl Marx wrote, 'The philosophers have only inter-
preted the world in various ways. The point, however,
is to change it.' And though much of what Marx
predicted hasn't come to pass, there was still a lot of
wisdom in his work. For example, he wrote in the
essay 'The Eighteenth Brumaire of Louis Napoleon':
'History repeats itself, first as tragedy, then as farce,
then an hour later it's repeated on ITV4+1 starring a
very young-looking Lewis Collins.'

GOLLUM'S GRANDAD

Newspapers used to have an enormous amount of
power to form opinion, didn't they? Particularly
columnists. As somebody who doesn't believe
almost anything said by anybody about anything,
I used to have an inordinate amount of respect for
columns and columnists. The journalists who write
them always seem to speak with such certainty. One
columnist would thunder, 'Being left wing gives you
cancer!' and I would think, Oh yeah, that's right, I
think it does. Then another would say, 'Being right
wing gives you cancer!' and I would believe them
completely. Then I noticed after a while that it was
the same columnist who was saying both things!
A few months apart! And I realised they were just
pretending to have all these opinions because they

have to knock out three columns a week. They are completely insincere; it is all just a pretence.

I was also strongly influenced by critics, particularly those who wrote such things as, 'This film marks a stonking return to form by Woody Allen.' Which is why I've seen so many shit Woody Allen films. 'Oh like, this one, oh right this one, is about a seventeen- year-old girl who falls for, like, a ninety-year-old man who looks like Gollum's grandad. But this one, it's set in Rome.'

Then I thought to myself, Boris Johnson was a columnist, wasn't he? For years he was a columnist on the *Telegraph* while Michael Gove was one for *The Times* and Michael Gove's wife was too and they are just people for whom words mean nothing. They change their opinions at the drop of a hat and they never admit that they once pretended to believe the exact opposite of what they're pretending to believe in right now.

Yet somehow they get away with it. When Boris Johnson was editor of the *Spectator*, his office was in my street and sometimes he used to stop and chat to me, and Boris exuded such upper-class charm, he had such a smooth manner that even I used to come over all proletarian in his presence. I used to start speaking in a weird overawed voice saying, 'Ooh Mr Johnson, ooh yer hair, ooh yer beautiful golden hair, oooh insult me in French, Mr Johnson. Say something in Greek, Mr Johnson. Something profound in Greek that you learnt at Oxford, Mr Johnson...' And I began to develop this fantasy about me and Boris. I began to fantasise that we were soldiers together in the First World War. I was a humble squaddie, a simple private but with a nice tanned muscular body and I think a kind of ambiguous sexuality. And Boris would be an officer, I think he'd be a good officer; he'd make sure his men had decent boots and reasonable food and he'd make sure that all the poets had fresh pencils.

So it's late 1917, dawn, just before the big push in my fantasy. We're in the trench all lined up and Boris is in the front and we're all behind him and then a flare goes up and explodes in the sky – 'Poof!' – turning night into day and Boris blows a whistle and we go up the ladders and over the top and Boris is leading and we're following, then the German machine guns open up and the bullets are zipping past us, but Boris is leading we're following, even though our comrades are falling to left and right then the whizz-bangs start exploding in the sky and the shrapnel is ripping the flesh of our fellow soldiers but Boris is leading and we're following, then the heavy artillery starts coming down and there's great gouts of mud and flesh and bone but

Boris is leading and we're following and then we get to the barbed wire and at the first opportunity I shoot him in the back and I try and defect to the Soviet Union!

Chapter Three

PROFESSIONAL WOMAN, MID-THIRTIES
When you are doing publicity for a book or a radio series, one of your tasks is to answer questionnaires in newspapers and magazines. These have names such as 'A Day in the Life', 'Five Minutes With...' or 'My London' and the answers are often given over the phone. Over the years I have, perhaps mistakenly, tried to be funny in these questionnaires. This is from the *Telegraph* a few years ago:

Question: Which of your possessions would you be unable to live without?
To which I've replied: My kidney dialysis machine.
Then question: How would you describe yourself in a Lonely Hearts column?

And I've said: Professional woman, mid-thirties, interested in being taken to all-you-can-eat buffets in the West Midlands area.

Question: Do you believe people can achieve anything if they set their minds to it?

Answer: No, you can't even get somebody to take you to an all-you-can-eat buffet in the West Midlands area, no matter how hard you try.

Question: What's the best way to mend a broken heart?

Answer: Taking a nice, slightly hairy professional woman to an all-you-can-eat buffet in the West Midlands area.

There was one of those questionnaires I did for the *London Evening Standard* and I was asked: How do you escape?

And again trying to be funny I replied: I knot some sheets together and I climb out the window.

However, when the piece was printed they'd changed the question to: How do you chill out?

One of the standard enquiries they make around Christmas time is: What is your New Year's resolution? I always reply: United Nations Resolution 242, the one that calls for a homeland for the Palestinian people. I sense the poor intern on the other end of the line rolling their eyes as I say this.

There is a story I heard about the British ambassador in Washington in the 1980s. On Christmas Eve he was rung by a TV station and asked what he'd like for Christmas. Worried about bribery and corruption and accepting gifts from a foreign TV network, he replied, 'Ooh, um, er... just a small box of chocolates.' On Christmas Day the ambassador was watching the news and at the end of the main TV bulletin the newsreader said, 'And finally we asked the ambassadors of several countries what they wanted for Christmas. The French ambassador said world peace, the Soviet ambassador said an end to hunger and the British ambassador said a small box of chocolates...'

But making a New Year's resolution is something I have intermittently tried to do. The resolution I have adhered to the most over the decades since I made it in the 1990s is to wave at more people. I am a big fan of waving. I was first introduced to waving by my father. As a child waiting on a railway platform with my dad I'd be urged to wave at the train guard of any express or freight train that went past. The first hint of the complexities of adult nature came to me when I suddenly realised that Joe, my father, was a train guard himself! Then I wondered if all train guards didn't have a pact to encourage their sons and daughters to salute them, perhaps as a part of their ongoing war with train drivers, who they thought were very up themselves.

Nonetheless to this day I remain very keen on waving. I still salute passing trains but also passengers on river boats, racing cyclists, police officers on horses (but not ordinary police officers) and airline pilots waiting on the stand to start their engines.

Over the years I have done a lot of motoring journalism and one summer I was testing a new car with a long drive down to the South of France. As we passed through a small Pyrenean village there was a man standing on a corner and the driver in front of us, presumably a local, tooted his horn at this man who waved back enthusiastically, so I did the same and again the man waved back with vigour, a big smile on his face, then as we neared I saw a look of confusion cross his countenance. I think about this man often. I wonder if he remains unsettled by the fact that he knows somebody who drives a 2006 Kia Magentis on UK plates but he's never found out who they are and this makes the world feel a much more frightening and insecure place.

One vehicle I've found out it is a bad idea to salute is that sinister black-windowed van that ships prisoners to and from the law courts. You'd think the people in the back of those things would be glad of a friendly wave as they begin a long sentence, but some of them turn out to be very bad-tempered individuals indeed, with surprisingly loud voices, enabling their disturbing obscenities and violent threats to be heard clearly through the walls of the van.

MY GIRLFRIEND

(Just to give you a warning, this section may contain words that try and replicate the sounds of flash photography.) Susan Sarandon, the American actress and activist who's starred in such films *The Rocky Horror Picture Show*, *Thelma & Louise*, *The Witches of Eastwick* and *The Lovely Bones*, was in my shop for her regular bacon roll with a side order of another bacon roll.

She's my girlfriend. Except I think she's been cheating on me with Liam Dutton, who presents the weather on Channel 4 News. Scrircht! Kaflash! Whoomp! Maybe I'm not treating her right but I'm trying. Last week I took her to see Jethro Tull, not the 1970s psychedelic band but the eighteenth-century agronomist, horticulturalist and inventor of the seed drill. Man, he rocked! Then we went to a concert, a performance of the *1812 Overture* with real cannons but also with real cholera and real flesh wounds.

(Just to break the fourth wall for a moment here. It is true that I live in the next street to Channel 4 News and I do sometimes see Liam Dutton walking towards or leaving the building and I am often tempted to shout at him, 'Oi you, Dutton. Leave my bird alone!' But I'm not sure if he's heard of his part in my radio show; he might just think it's some kind of racial or anti-weatherman incident.)

BOINGIO

Now you will have noticed from a lot of my replies to that questionnaire that I have something of an obsession with all-you-can-eat buffets. This is because I think all-you-can-eat buffets are a very good metaphor for capitalism. With capitalism we are encouraged to believe that it's not any of the things we already own that will make us happy but it will be the very next thing we buy that will tip us over into a profound state of bliss. The next phone or flat-screen TV or hideous disfiguring tattoo or dangerous dog, that's the thing that's going to make us endlessly content. So when I'm in the Chinese all-you-can-eat buffet, I'm not thinking about what's on my plate but instead about the next thing I'm going to eat, so my mind is going, Oh yeah, these barbecue ribs are good but those Vietnamese paper-wrapped prawns I'm going to have next, wow, it's going to be like there's a lavish party in my mouth and Sir Philip Green isn't invited!

Now, I do this terrible thing when I'm in a Chinese restaurant. I can't speak Chinese, but I don't want to be a tourist, an outsider, I want to seem worldly wise and sophisticated, so what I do is I put on a Chinese accent. It's not a racist accent, it's the accent of an older man from Guangzhou Province, a wealthy individual, sophisticated, owner of an electronics company, educated at a Western university, MIT or UCLA.

So I'm looking at the menu and I'm going, 'Ahhh ... gimme the mixed-meat fried noodle and ahhh ... the hot an' sour soup ... the boil rice, an' uh yah, I'll have the roast duck on the de ... boil rice ...'

No, you're right, even in print it is racist.

It's considered a sign of intelligence, isn't it, to be fluent in languages, but then Jim Davidson speaks really good English, so I'm not so sure. It was an assumption in our family that we were all really good at speaking foreign languages but it was a lie. Because my dad worked on the railways we travelled all over Europe for free and Joe, my dad, supposedly spoke this language called Esperanto. This was one of those things invented in the early twentieth century that were supposed to make the world a better place ... like Fascism. Esperanto as spoken by my father seemed to consist mostly of bits of French, Spanish, German and English and the word 'boingio'. So he'd be like, 'Me gusto boingio una sandwich boingio de jamon unt fromage boingio.' While my mother supposedly spoke Yiddish, which was sort of similar to German, but in reality she just screamed at people until they did what she wanted.

So, anyway, my hobby has been, for years, to find the cheapest all-you-can-eat buffet in Britain. And finally I found it. Surprisingly it was in Islington, an Indian vegetarian restaurant in Chapel Market, Islington. And at the time it was all-you-can-eat Indian vegetarian food for £2.95. They did things like curried sprouts. A lot of the people in there seemed to be wearing those paper jumpsuits the police give you when you've been sick on yourself in the cells. And a lot of the other customers were Jeremy Corbyn.

So I wrote an article in *The Times* about the place and the next time I went in there the owner said to me, 'Oh Mr Sayle, thank you for writing that article about my restaurant in the papers. No no,' he said, 'no no, please, let me pay for your lunch.' And I thought, Bloody hell, every man's got his price; it turns out mine is £2.95!

When I first appeared on the TV back in the early 1980s, people used to send letters to the BBC and make phone calls, reviewers would write articles in the papers saying things like, 'What is this man doing on the television? He's crazy, his routines don't make any kind of sense, it's all just swearing and shouting and yelling about Bertolt Brecht and Albania!' And of course they were right but the reason I remained on the TV nonetheless was because I'm a Freemason. I attended Chelsea Art School in the 1970s and, just like the South Yorkshire Police Force, all the London art schools at that time were a hotbed of Freemasonry.

In the 1990s, though, I disappeared from the TV screens and was forced to become a writer and that was because I was thrown out of the Freemasons for breaking the rules. You remember before the millennium how people used to go over to France just to buy booze? Wine, beer and spirits were a lot cheaper on the Continent, so you got these huge booze supermarkets on the outskirts of Calais and Boulogne. But what is less well known is that it was also possible to buy Masonic regalia much cheaper in France, so there were these big regalia super-markets and they didn't just do Masonic stuff; you could buy Jewish yarmulkes and those big furry hats that the Lubavitchers wear, complete ayatollah outfits and Catholic gear up to the rank of cardinal. Indeed, they were a place of peace: Muslim and Jew, Protestant and Catholic, Buddhist and Hindu, Yazidi and Zoroastrian all mixed together without enmity because they were focused on what united them, not what divided them, which was the great savings to be made on giant crucifixes and hijabs. So I used to load the car up with aprons, silver-plated set squares, goblets, white gloves and medallions at a quarter of the cost I'd pay in the UK, then bring it all back and sell it to other chaps who were 'on the square', but then the big bosses found out about it and I was expelled from the Masons. It was really only when I joined the Taliban that my career revived.

'They were all focused on what united them, not what divided them'

Both my parents were in an organisation that was in some ways very similar and in some ways very different from the Freemasons. They were members of the British Communist Party; they told me it was Lenin who came down the chimney at Christmas! Them being in this authoritarian organisation gave me a lifelong distrust of leaders of political parties, those psychopaths and people with personality disorders who force themselves to the top of any grouping or organisation.

I was on *The Andrew Marr Show* a few years ago reviewing the papers and one of the other guests was the then leader of the Labour Party Ed Miliband and I was a bit worried about meeting him but he came up to me and he said, 'Bloody hell!', he said. 'Alexei bloody Sayle!' Oddly enough, just like the Earl of Sandwich, Ed Miliband talks in a thick Scouse accent. So it would be best if you imagine his words spoken by footballer Wayne Rooney or the late Cilla Black. He's like, 'I'm bleeding Ed Miliband, I'm leader of the Labour Party, I get forty per cent off in Yates's Wine Lodge. See these trainies, see these trainies? I robbed them off Vince Cable ...'

But you see, one of the problems Ed Miliband had was his advisers wouldn't let him be himself.

So anyway, Ed Miliband says to me, 'Alexei Sayle, it's great to meet you, do you know it's exactly twenty-five years ago today since the release of your hit single "Ullo John! Gotta New Motor?"? We were huge fans of that song in our house.' And I had this impression of him in his Hampstead Marxist home, him and his brother David, his father Ralph scrawling 'I hate Britain' in his own excrement on the walls, and all their left-wing friends – Tariq Ali and Germaine Greer and Noam Chomsky – and they're all going, '"Ullo John! Gotta new motor? Ullo John! Gotta new motor?"' So I was really charmed by him but then a few minutes later I thought, Hang on, exactly twenty-five years ago today? Even I didn't know it was exactly twenty-five years ago today, then I thought what he'd done was he'd gone to one of his assistants and he'd said, "Ere … Google that twat, will you?'

EL DORADO

I came from that generation of working-class kids from the 1960s for whom, through full grants and all our fees paid, the gates of El Dorado the Golden, City briefly swung open and via university places and going to art school or drama school we subsequently got great jobs in the media and the arts. Those gates are firmly slammed shut again. Until recently the Labour Party, which was supposed to represent the interests of working-class kids, had become firmly dynastic. Neil Kinnock's son Stephen Kinnock is an MP, Tony Benn's son Hilary Benn is an MP, Jack Straw's son Kim Jong Straw...

(Hello, it's me again, breaking the fourth wall. I notice in his columns recently the *Guardian's* sketch writer John Crace has been calling Theresa May 'Kim Jong May' which is similar to my Kim Jong Straw gag but I can produce receipts and CCTV footage that prove I've been doing that gag since at least 2012.)

You know, one of the things it's very difficult for me to do on my radio show is any really topical material because there's such a big time gap between recording the show and it being transmitted. The reason for this is that the BBC has such a backlog of absolutely fantastic comedy shows, which need to be broadcast before mine can go out.

So I made the first series of *Imaginary Sandwich Bar* in March 2009. But the earliest we could get a transmission date was November 2016. I didn't know what was going to happen between recording and transmission. Obviously I knew Gordon Brown was going to get re-elected with a landslide majority but apart from that I had to guess.

The Conservative Party, despite its recent reshuffles, is still stacked with people who went to public school and either Oxford or Cambridge and it still very much serves the ruling class. In the 1960s and 1970s all the great British movie stars were working class – Albert Finney, Michael Caine, Tom Courtenay, Peter O'Toole – now they've all been to public school and Oxbridge. Damian Lewis, Tom Hiddleston, Dominic West, Benedict Cumberbatch and Eddie Redmayne all went to either Eton or Harrow, and they are now starting to colonise the few decent jobs that they used to leave for the working class, like you're getting all these posh comedians now. Like Jack Whitehall, who went to Marlborough, or Miranda Hart, who went to Downe House. Footballers! Leicester City striker Jamie Vardy went to Winchester and All Souls College, Oxford! Explorers! Bloody explorers! Public schoolboy Bear Grylls. What a phoney! He's not a bear and he's not a grill! Burger vans! Burger vans! All the burger vans down my local market are run by the class of Charterhouse of 2005! Mexican street food, for God's sake! Mexican street food chain Wahaca is not owned and run by a poor but honest man called Pedro from Guadalajara but privately educated Thomasina Miers, who comes from Cheltenham! And there's a pop-up Vietnamese pho café in Peckham High Street that's run by the Queen and Prince Philip!

HALFPRICEMASONS
In a way though it is deplorable it's sort of human nature that people combine together in self-serving cabals like the Freemasons. The comedy mafia in the UK is nicknamed the Laffia. The Scottish mafia, which is powerful in the media north of the border, is referred to as the Mackia, while the corresponding Welsh mafia is called the Taffia, and the Italian mafia is called the Mafia.

Mind you, I sometimes wonder what we gained, us bright, working-class kids, by getting to see El Dorado because in a sense we lost our tribe, we became deracinated. In a way we were no longer authentically working class but we were nothing else. A friend of mine, Terry, after his first couple of terms at art school came home for the holidays and he was sitting in the front room with his dad and they could both sense that something irrevocable had shifted between them, something had changed for ever, something that they could never get back, and there was this uneasy silence between them until finally Terry's dad looked up from the paper and he said, 'So, Terry, what do you fancy for the National?'

'Well...' Terry replied. 'Peter Hall's production of *Troilus and Cressida*...'

POSH HIPPY ENTREPRENEURS

I was doing a book reading a while back and in the question-and-answer session I was amazed to chance upon an enormous amount of hatred for James Dyson. Perhaps there's something about the self-congratulatory nature of his vacuum cleaners – 'Ooh look at me, I'm bagless but I'm in bright colours!' – that enrages people. I don't know. Whereas there was a great deal of affection for those

Henry vacuum cleaners because they've got a face on them.

But the phenomenon of the posh hippy entrepreneur such as James Dyson or Richard Branson: they put themselves at the forefront of their products, which is a relatively new thing, isn't it? And their hippy credentials, I think, are often false. Like Ben and Jerry of Ben & Jerry's ice cream, they actually met in Vietnam when they were both in the Green Berets. A lot of their early flavours had names such as Napalm Nut Cluster, Agent Orange and Die, You VC Gook, Die!

THE REST IS GEOGRAPHY

There's this TV channel called Yesterday; it's a history sort of channel, but when it first appeared on Freeview for some reason it used to go off the air at 6.30 in the evening, at which point they'd put up a sign on the screen that said: 'Yesterday will be back tomorrow.'

Of course when I started out in TV there were only three channels, which then expanded to four. Whereas now there are all these new outlets, not just all the stations on Freeview and cable, but Netflix and Amazon. Which is good, because a working-class entertainer like me is being forced off the main channels by all the posh Jack Whitehalls and Miranda

Harts but I'm actually working on a new comedy series which will be shown exclusively on ITV2+1. It's absolutely brilliant, but you will never see it because it will always appear one hour into the future.

DANCE, DIEGO, DANCE!

Of course the upper classes were never ever truly going to accept us bright working-class kids, even a class traitor like Bryan Ferry; when he rides out with his local fox hunt, they're all making 'wanker' gestures behind his back.

They were never going to accept us because, let's face it, rich people are horrible! That is not a value judgement, that is simply evolutionary science, because poor people, they need to be nice to each other, like you need to be nice to your mate because one day you might want to borrow his van. But Roman Abramovich, he's got his own van! A 2014 Renault Trafic, air conditioning, satnav and Bluetooth. Roman Abramovich, he's like, 'Ha ha ha, I've got all the cheese in the world, ha ha ha! Now I'm going to get Diego Costa to come round to my house and dance about in his underpants! Ha ha ha. Dance, Diego, dance! Dance, you petulant-Brazilian-slash–Spanish man-child, dance! Now I'll get John Terry to come in and say something racist! That's what it's like in Belgravia!

Perhaps the one person, certainly the one political leader who embodies everything that is noble and honest and staying true to yourself, is Nelson Mandela. I actually met Nelson Mandela in 1992, not long after he'd been released from prison, a while before he was elected president of South Africa. I'd done some benefit gigs for the ANC and so they invited me to meet him at this small reception at a hotel in central London. And I got really nervous about meeting Nelson Mandela, I thought, What if I meet him and he's not admirable, what if I meet him and he's got the cold dead eyes of the professional revolutionary, the cold dead eyes and the wet handshake of the kind of men who used to come to Communist Party meetings in our front room and eat all the bleeding biscuits! And by the time I got to meet Nelson Mandela I was so nervous that I couldn't speak. But luckily Nelson Mandela took my hand in his and he said, 'Bloody hell!' he said. 'Alexei Sayle! Do you know it's exactly eight years ago today since the release of your hit single "Ullo John! Gotta New Motor?"? We loved that song on Robben Island.'

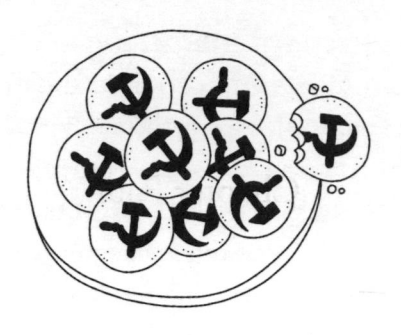

The kind of men who used to come to Communist Party meetings in our front room and eat all the bleeding biscuits!

Chapter Four

A SPECIAL GIFT

I know someone who is very good at giving presents. She is assiduous about remembering when everybody's birthday or anniversary occurs and then handing them the perfect gift, beautifully wrapped with a nice little card containing a witty personalised message. I am not like that, I rarely give any sort of present to anybody, though this is not just due to meanness or my lack of social grace but it is also because I am traumatised by the memory of the terrible damage a poorly thought-out present can cause.

I once had two friends, a couple called Mike and Sue. On the occasion of their tenth wedding anniversary one of Mike's old schoolfriends, now the manager of a successful rock band, gave them a very expensive gift. It was basically a book of vouchers that entitled them to dine at all kinds of smart restaurants, go on sailing holidays, enjoy beauty treatments and many more wonderful experiences of all kinds. The only catch was that it was basically a two-for-one offer, so if Mike and Sue dined at the Ritz say, then Mike would eat for free but Sue would have to pay the full cost of everything, or if they took the seats at the opera then again one of them would be paying nothing but the other would be paying quite a lot. Nevertheless, though they were not free, the vouchers in this book offered the couple an entry to all kinds of exclusive places and experiences that they could not normally have dreamed of enjoying.

However, Mike and Sue soon found that when they had a bit of free time they did not necessarily want to dine at the Ritz on the chef's table or go rock climbing, even if accompanied by Bear Grylls. But if the couple went out somewhere and the place was not in their book of two-for-one vouchers, they suffered a tremendous amount of guilt and anger because they were paying the maximum price, yet if they did visit a place that was included in their book of coupons they were consumed with a murderous rage at being forced into going somewhere they didn't really want to go.

Slowly the pair stopped going out altogether and after work remained in their flat with the curtains closed and the lights off in case Mike's old school-friend was passing and saw that they weren't out enjoying his gift. This meant that they began to get on each other's nerves and in time Sue came to blame Mike for having such a thoughtless friend who would give them this poisoned offering. They turned in on themselves, horizons narrowed and from there it was only a short time until both of them fell into depression and despair.

Finally, in an act of desperation, the couple took out the volume of vouchers, which to them had come to resemble a book of evil spells, and from its depths they booked a hot-air-balloon flight over the scenic Cotswolds.

On a sunny Sunday morning, once the craft had reached a sufficient height, the couple threw themselves out of the basket. Well one of them did.

OUR COUNTRY'S FAIRLY OK

Tonight I want to talk about history and the role of entertainment and the entertainer in society. Audiences for classical music and theatre audiences think they're superior to stand-up comedy audiences but I'm not so sure. A few years ago my wife went to a performance of a play called *Our Country's Good* written by a woman called Timberlake Wertenbaker and after the play had finished, as they were filing out, she heard a woman in front of her say, 'Oh, I was at school with a Timberlake Wertenbaker, I wonder if it's the same one.'

You hear people misusing language these days, don't you? They say '*mano a mano*' thinking it means 'man to man' when in fact it means 'hand to hand', since speaking Spanish isn't about just putting an 'o' at the end of English words. And I heard a sports commentator say on TV the other day, 'It's time to batter down the hatches.' What does that mean, 'batter down the hatches'? Like people say 'a damp squid'. I mean all squids are damp!

I was somewhere and one of our party said something obvious and another person in response said, 'No shit, Shylock!' I mean what would you say that would be obvious to a seventeenth-century Venetian Jew?

2.22, 5.55

When I was about fifteen I discovered, in a tatty little second-hand bookshop in my neighbourhood of Anfield, a box of these pulpy, square little magazines some merchant seaman presumably had brought over from the United States. They had names such as *Astounding Science Fiction, Galaxy Science Fiction* and *If.* The owner wanted a shilling per copy, which I eagerly paid, and each proved to be a box of treasures, short stories, novellas, many written by the masters of the genre, Philip K. Dick (*The Man in the High Castle, Do Androids Dream of Electric Sheep?*), Ray Bradbury (*Fahrenheit 451, I Sing the Body Electric*) and Richard Matheson (*I Am Legend*, 'Duel'). I remember reading one story that has stayed with me to this day. It concerned a man who, when he was sleeping, would sometimes come to in the middle of the night with that familiar sensation of being up in the air then, in the split second before truly waking, plunge back down to the bed. Anyway it turned out that the sensation wasn't an illusion and he was in fact flying and I can't recall what happened in the story after that.

I now believe I'm having a similar experience. Though my sleep is heavy, I've got into the habit of half-waking every few hours and looking at the lit-up clock on the bedside table to see what time it is. Now generally the clock shows a normal hour, 1.27 or 4.38, but more often than I think can possibly be explained by coincidence, the screen displays the same three identical numbers such as 2.22, 3.33 or 5.55. (I also think that on one occasion it read 7.77, but on the other hand I did get very drunk the night before.) What I take from these numbers on my clock is that life is a giant fabrication, as in the movie *The Adjustment Bureau* (based on a Philip K. Dick story),where there is no free will and all human life is controlled by mysterious men in natty hats. The operatives who are in charge of maintaining the illusion that our world is real during the day are highly competent. They never let slip for a second any hint that things are not as we believe they are. The night-time crew are another matter; they are the sort of people who staff petrol stations and convenience stores in the early hours or who you find on the night bus, inattentive, hung-over, resentful, a bit weird and they don't always do such a good job. Most obviously they are supposed to make sure that time continues to run forwards while everybody sleeps, but sometimes they are out the back of the control room having a fag or they themselves have nodded off, and so time stalls and the clocks freeze on a default setting, hence the identical numbers. So that's it, our world is a chimera and a mysterious organisation controls what we do, for our own good. I certainly hope that's the case or we're all fucked.

THE CHIEF RABBI'S BASEBALL CAP

I'm sixty-five now. They say you know you're getting old when policemen start to look young to you. My mate Harry says you know you're getting old when the chief rabbi starts looking young to you. But this business of getting older is a strange thing. For me it's amazing how much history I've lived through. Like a lot's changed since I invented alternative comedy. One of the things that's distressed me is the role of the topical TV comedy panel show in the rehabilitation of the reputations of war criminals. When I say war criminals I mean people like John Prescott and Alastair Campbell, people who led us into two illegal wars in which hundreds of thousands, possibly millions, of people have died. I mean if Joseph Goebbels was alive today he wouldn't be on trial at Nuremberg, he'd be hosting *Have I Got News for You*! At least when she lost power Thatcher had the good grace to slink off into an alcoholic haze but people like Alastair Campbell and Ed Balls will do anything to remain in the public eye! 'Alastair Campbell talks movingly on *Panorama* about his depression...' Of course you're depressed, you bastard, you're a mass murderer! Doesn't matter how many marathons you run, you'll never get away from your conscience! It's *Three Bastards in a Boat*: Griff Rhys Jones, Rory McGrath and Robert Mugabe! Tonight on *Strictly Come Dancing* we've got Freddie Flintoff, Emily Maitlis and Radovan Karadžić, the Butcher of Bosnia!

Now, lots of people, like my girlfriend Susan Sarandon, have said to me, 'Alexei, you like dancing, you should go on *Strictly Come Dancing*, you should, *Strictly* you should, go on.' And Yo-Yo Ma, even he's going, 'You should go on *Strictly*, Alexei.' And Neil Kinnock, he's going, 'Yeah, you should go on *Strictly*.' And Professor Green, he's going, 'You should, you should go on *Strictly*, Alexei.' And Shinzō Abe, the prime minister of Japan, he's going, 'Yeah, you should go on, you should go on *Strictly*, Alexei.'

A lot's changed since I invented alternative comedy

Now I do like dancing, I can salsa as well as any north London social worker, but I will never go on *Strictly*. First of all I hate all TV talent shows such as *The X Factor* and *Britain's Got Talent*. It was my distant relation, filmmaker Albert Maysles, who stated, 'Tyranny is the removal of nuance.'

Which brings us to *Strictly* ... Everything is wrong with ballroom dancing: the clothes, the music, even the expressions on the dancers' faces, plus of course the dancing itself. The reason for this is simple – you get points for it. Ballroom dancing is an aesthetic pursuit, an art form, which has been turned into a competition, the result of which is that everything is done to attract the attention of the judges. The competitors must try to fit in to a set of rules rather than display emotion, artistry and invention, and so a tawdry, flashy, kitsch aesthetic takes over. Imagine if actors got points for doing Shakespeare what kind of overblown, hammy performances you would get. If you see a couple performing a proper Argentinian tango you are watching a dance created in the brothels of Buenos Aires that reeks of melancholy and sex. Then you watch the ballroom version of tango, all gurning faces and robotic, angular, hideous movements. You are seeing a great popular art reduced to a terrible travesty.

Now obviously dance is not revolutionary in itself, indeed I believe that no art can directly affect politics. It's a mistake to think that it can.

I think the best thing about comedy affecting politics was said by Peter Cook when he opened the Establishment in Soho in the 1960s. He said he wanted his club to resemble those German cabaret clubs that appeared during the Weimar Republic and that did so much to stop the rise of Hitler.

But what the celebrities who appear on *Strictly* are doing is they are taking part in the ongoing cultural war on critical thinking. Just as in Orwell's *1984* where War is Peace, Freedom is Slavery, so in *Strictly*, Ugliness is Beauty, Prancing About is Dancing and Len Goodman isn't a leathery old cockney idiot. The end result of all this is that when people are confronted by the truth, they cannot see it because they have been so confused by lies. But don't let that stop you enjoying it.

A MESSAGE TO THE PEOPLE OF BRITAIN
Here, I'll tell you what I hate ... Fascism! I can't stand it, me, I think it's really, really terrible. I do. I think its bang out of order. That's just me, though. You might like it, you might think it's OK. Indeed, you might be a fan of radical authoritarian nationalism but I think you'd be wrong.

You see, I am able to have insights like that because I've had a long life and also, unlike a lot of comedians, I actually have had a very wide education. My original background is in science; for my first degree I studied in France at their famous research institute the Laboratoire Garnier under the renowned Nazi professor, Dr Oetker. Dr Oetker actually got off light at the Nuremberg war trials because he did all the catering.

Then unlike most leftists I also have a background in business and I actually know quite a lot about how the stock markets behave. I used to trade in Near East long-term debt derivatives, trading ratios on the Frankfurt DAX Exchange ... but I pulled out because it all became too commercial.

The philosopher George Santayana, before he founded his Latino-influenced guitar band, said, 'Those who forget the lessons of history are condemned to repeat them.' This seems to have been adopted by Western governments as a policy strategy.

One of the problems with the way we in the West receive our current affairs is that each broadcast or article, whether in old media or on the web, is totally without context – each story acts as if history began last Tuesday and not a day before. This of course tends to favour our own self-pitying view of ourselves as victims of random and incomprehensible violence from 'the Other'. From my life experience I would propose that all news stories concerning the Middle East would have to go back as far as the Sykes–Picot Agreement of 1916, a shameful time when we betrayed the Arab nations to whom we and the French had promised independence, while every fifth piece would have to go all the way back to the Crusades to provide vital historical context, and every news story concerning China would be required to include a lengthy section about the Opium Wars when Britain forced the drug on the reluctant Chinese. All this context would mean that each edition of *Newsnight* would be eleven hours long instead of just feeling like it's eleven hours long, and each article ... would be the length of a novel, but that sadly would be the price we'd have to pay to be well informed.

A MERRY COMMUNIST CHRISTMAS

When I was a kid, given that we were two thirds Jewish atheist Communists, Christmas was a surprisingly important occasion in our house. On British television, during the 1950s and 1960s, the holiday period was also a time when presentations from the Soviet Union were prominently featured. It was as if there was considered to be something seasonal about performances originating from a godless, authoritarian dictatorship.

I suppose that they felt that Santa was a lot like Stalin

The Moscow State Circus, with its spectacularly unfunny clowns, disturbingly dangerous high-wire acts and animal cruelty, would be transmitted live and at interminable length from a tent in Manchester. Now one of the things you have to remember about my parents, particularly my mother, is that they believed, being Communists, that anything from the Soviet Union was superior to anything from the West, so, 'Best horsemen in the world,' my mother Molly would say with a tremble of pride in her voice, referring to the Cossack horsemen who leapt on and off the backs of their stocky ponies as they hurtled round and round the circus ring. Presumably these men were the direct descendants of those Cossacks who had set fire to her grandmother's village. 'Oh yes,' she would say, 'best Jew-murderers in the world ...

ooh if you want a pogrom organising, get yerself a Cossack.'

How long you live is not what killed your parents but what killed your grandparents … so I should live for ever, as long as I don't bump into any Russian Cossacks. Which basically means not going round Knightsbridge or Chelsea. Many of the flats in those neighbourhoods are now used exclusively to house the ponies of wealthy Cossack oligarchs.

The Bolshoi Ballet, too, was a regular fixture of the holiday period and I can vividly recall sitting on the couch, jammed in between my parents Molly and Joe, as they fell asleep the moment the programme began, leaving me to watch three hours of *Swan Lake* to the accompaniment of stentorian snoring.

My parents, though, were always remarkably keen to take me to see Santa at his grotto in Lewis's department store in central Liverpool. I suppose that they felt that Santa was a lot like Stalin. Their names were sort of similar and they were both kindly looking, rotund gentlemen with facial hair and red uniforms whose headquarters were located in the northern snowy wastes and were based upon a system of slave labour.

At first we would shop for my presents at something called the Daily Worker Bazaar which was held at the Communist Party bookshops. On long trestle tables would be arrayed sickly pot plants, Marxist literature, Paul Robeson records and crudely carved wooden toys from East Germany and dolls from the Soviet Union, which when you unscrewed them sometimes contained scribbled notes from Aleksandr Solzhenitsyn begging to be released from the gulag.

I THOUGHT HE WAS MY FRIEND BUT HE WASN'T

It's amazing how the world has changed even in my lifetime. When I was young you'd see these signs on flats for rent that would say: 'No Dogs, No Blacks, No Irish'. Which was terrible, though it always bothered me why dogs were trying to rent their own apartments!

This is a personal thing, but I'll tell you, there's one working dog that I can't stand and that's that sniffer dog at the airport. He acts all friendly, doesn't he? He acts like he's your mate, you know, with his waggly tail, but really he's just a nark, he's a snitch, he's a graaass! He just wants to find out if you're carrying your lucky hand grenade onto the aeroplane.

A few years ago a friend of mine was going through a US airport and she's an animal lover and she bent down to pat the sniffer dog on the head. And immediately the dog's handler began to draw his weapon and shouted, 'Step away from the federal officer, ma'am!'

Undoubtedly, especially over the last 150 years or so, people's life expectancy in the industrialised nations has got much, much longer. But does it mean that because we are living longer we are enjoying the extra time that we've gained? For example, nowadays we get really narked and frustrated if we are held up on a car journey for a mere few minutes, and an hour or two sends us completely crackers, yet in the past when people's lives were very much shorter they didn't seem to mind spending a much greater proportion of them on journeys.

This is a press handout from Thames Trains. In the seventeenth century when most human beings only lasted into their forties, three years to sail to India and back on the off chance of seeing a new kind of fish wasn't a problem; in the eighteenth century nine months to walk to Italy to buy a special sort of leather hat was considered a cool thing to do; and in Charles Dickens's time four days on the stagecoach from Swindon to London to take your shoes to a bloke in Cheapside who wasn't a particularly good cobbler, well why not? And interruptions to the journey would be taken in your stride: held captive by Levantine brigands for a decade on the road to Samarkand? When you got back, your family would say they hadn't noticed you'd popped out.

OBSERVATIONS ON THE FEELING OF THE BEAUTIFUL AND SUBLIME
I don't want to brag or anything but I can still get into the same pair of trousers that I was wearing thirty years ago. Mind you, I was attending clown college at the time!

THE LE CHRISTMAS PARTY
I've always had a wonderful working relationship with the Corporation. When it first went out, *The Young Ones* wasn't that popular, but the BBC, with its profound elephantine wisdom going back half a century knew it was going to be good and that year, even though it still hadn't really taken off, they invited the cast to the Light Entertainment Christmas Party – a real vote of confidence. No younger comedians had been invited to the LE Christmas Party, the high point of the year for all comedians, comic actors and sex offenders, since a dark day in the 1970s when the Pythons had been asked to this black-tie event and had turned up dressed in jeans!

I felt it was a sign that the BBC believed that acts like me, despite all the references to Marxism and Brecht and the left-wing propaganda, were still in many ways conventional show-business turns. I didn't wear a tuxedo but did dress up in a smart suit and tie and tried very hard to behave myself. I nearly succeeded until the moment when Jim Moir, the head of Light Entertainment, came over to me leading the Liverpool-born comic performer and radio DJ Kenny Everett. I bridled immediately. A few months previously, during a Young Conservatives rally held at Wembley Arena, Kenny had inflamed the reactionary, right-wing, tweed-jacketed crowd by coming on stage and shouting, 'Let's kick Michael Foot's stick away!' and, 'Let's bomb Russia!'

Jim said to me, 'You know who this is, don't you?'

'Yes,' I replied, turned and stalked off. My high-minded gesture was undermined by Kenny being way too stoned to notice what had happened and Jim assumed it was probably just some sort of a gay thing.

Later on Rowland Rivron showed his penis to Mrs Val Doonican in the lift. It was an indication of the corporation's priorities that all this was still considered better behaviour than the Pythons attending the Light Entertainment Christmas Party wearing jeans.

CLOSING TIME

So that's it, the end of another non-existent day at my imaginary sandwich bar. It's time to get into my van and drive home. Maybe my girlfriend Susan Sarandon will be in and we can have a nice evening free from recrimination and anger as long as nobody mentions weather forecasting.

There is a problem with me getting home, though. About a decade and a half ago an authoritative university report announced that in central London over a monitored period of five years the average speed of a car had dropped from eleven miles an hour to six miles an hour. Unfortunately this trend didn't stop there, it continued, and over the next few years, in the middle of the capital, traffic slowed down further and further, then eventually came to a complete halt. In keeping with the laws of physics there was a brief period when all vehicles remained absolutely motionless. Then all the cars, vans and trucks in London subsequently started to go backwards. Slowly at first, then faster and faster the vehicles went until now they are travelling at the speeds that they obtained before the war, but in reverse. So all those environmentalists were wrong: the problem of gridlock in our cities has been solved, that is as long as you don't mind travelling backwards and as long as you make certain you start your journey from the place where you were planning to go to in the first instance.

Goodbye everybody! Make good sandwich choices.

A Note on the Author

Born in Liverpool, the only child of Communist parents, Alexei Sayle moved to London in 1971 to attend Chelsea School of Art. He became the first MC of the Comedy Store and later the Comic Strip. After years of stand-up, television, sitcoms, films and even a hit single, he published his first highly acclaimed collection of short stories. *Barcelona Plates* was followed by *The Dog Catcher*, two novels: *Overtaken* and *The Weeping Women Hotel* and a novella, *Mister Roberts*. The first volume of Alexei's memoirs was *Stalin Ate My Homework*; the second, *Thatcher Stole My Trousers*.

alexeisayle.me

A Note on the Type

The text of this book is set Adobe Garamond. It is one of several versions of Garamond based on the designs of Claude Garamond. It is thought that Garamond based his font on Bembo, cut in 1495 by Francesco Griffo in collaboration with the Italian printer Aldus Manutius. Garamond types were first used in books printed in Paris around 1532. Many of the present-day versions of this type are based on the *Typi Academiae* of Jean Jannon cut in Sedan in 1615.

Claude Garamond was born in Paris in 1480. He learned how to cut type from his father and by the age of fifteen he was able to fashion steel punches the size of a pica with great precision. At the age of sixty he was commissioned by King Francis I to design a Greek alphabet, and for this he was given the honourable title of royal type founder. He died in 1561.